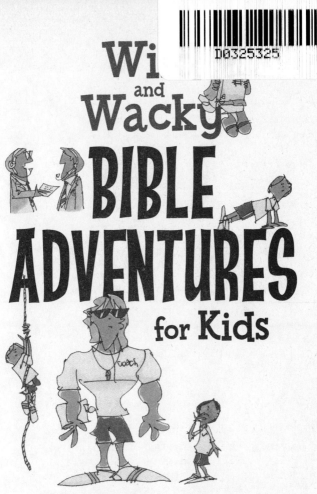

Wild and Wacky BIBLE ADVENTURES for Kids

Sandy Silverthorne

HARVEST HOUSE PUBLISHERS
EUGENE, OREGON

Cover by Left Coast Design, Portland, Oregon

WILD AND WACKY BIBLE ADVENTURES FOR KIDS
Formerly titled *The Awesome Book of Bible Stories for Kids*
Copyright © 2011 by Sandy Silverthorne
Published by Harvest House Publishers
Eugene, Oregon 97402
www.harvesthousepublishers.com

ISBN 978-0-7369-5673-4 (paperback)
ISBN 978-0-7369-5674-1 (eBook)

Printed in the United States of America

14 15 16 17 18 19 20 21 22 / BP-SK / 10 9 8 7 6 5 4 3 2 1

To my beautiful Vicki, whose encouragement
and laughter bless my life beyond measure;

to Christy, whose humor and grace are such gifts to so many,

and to the great kids I have the privilege
to speak to and share with.

You're the best!

Contents

Welcome to
Wild and Wacky Bible Adventures for Kids!

What if Gideon competed on a game show? What if John the Baptist sat in as a morning radio personality? Or what if Joshua's fight against Jericho inspired a video game? The Bible introduces us to some remarkable real-life people and amazing but true stories—giants who challenge God's people, everyday folks who become unlikely heroes, and one Guy who even controls the weather! We read about floods and battles and betrayals and people getting healed. It's all so exciting and real, you might feel like doing what Zacchaeus did—climbing up a tree so you can get a good look at Jesus.

This book presents some favorite Bible stories in modern settings and with some techno-gadgets and accessories you and I enjoy today. For example, nobody had a GPS in Moses' time. But what if he miraculously got his hands on one? Would that have helped him get to the Promised Land any sooner? And when David, the little shepherd boy from Bethlehem, fought the giant Goliath, TV cameras weren't there to broadcast the big event to the world. But what if a sports network had televised this incredible underdog success story? Would that be something worth playing on our TiVos over and over for our friends? Of course it would! See how fun it is to journey through the Bible with a time twist?

The stories in this book ask the question, what if? What if a weather network reported on Noah's flood? Or Joseph and his brothers appeared on a daytime talk show? Or Nehemiah rebuilt the Jerusalem wall on *Nehemiah's Extreme Makeover, Jerusalem Edition*? Our retellings of these stories will give you a laugh, and they will also give you a new perspective of what was really going on long ago. We hope you'll enjoy reading and discovering the lessons God wants all of us to learn.

Would you like to make this book even more fun? Get out your Bible and double-check to make sure just what really *did* happen in each of these accounts. To make that easier, the Scripture references are listed in the Get Real section following every story. So get ready to see what would have happened if...

1

What if an animal network filmed an episode in the Garden of Eden?

In the beginning God created the heavens and the earth. Think of it. He made everything—oceans, mountains, rivers, stars, planets, flowers, and every single animal. God made Adam and his wife, Eve, and placed them in the most beautiful spot on earth, the Garden of Eden.

One day, God gave Adam an assignment—to take care of the garden and tend the animals. He even let Adam come up with a name for each critter. But what if an animal network filmed a documentary in the Garden of Eden before Adam had a chance to name all the creatures? It might have looked something like this...

NARRATOR: The Garden of Eden—an incredible wonderland of waterfalls, lush green forests, deep clear pools, and emerald rolling hills. Everywhere you look, you see God's fingerprints, including thousands of beautiful plants and all kinds of animals living together in an oasis of splendid beauty. This is the beautiful spot where God chose to begin life on our planet.

NARRATOR: One majestic, four-footed creature surveys the landscape. This beautiful specimen silently pads through the underbrush. It truly is the king of beasts. In every way he lives up to his name of...uh, I'm not sure. What *is* his name? What do you call him, Adam?

ADAM: Hmmm. Haven't seen him before. Why don't we call him a lion? Yeah, that's good. Lion—I like the sound of that.

NARRATOR: This lion has three delightful little...?

ADAM: Cubs. Yeah, cubs. They look like cubs.

NARRATOR: They follow their father, imitating him and learning from him.

NARRATOR: Across the river is a...group?

ADAM: No, a *herd*...let's say herd.

NARRATOR: Okay, a herd of...

ADAM: Oh, I don't know...salamanders? No, not salamanders. How about giraffes? That sounds pretty good. And they are a bit funny looking! Yes—call them giraffes.

NARRATOR: And here we see a *baby* giraffe.

NARRATOR: The giraffes lead their baby to the watering hole, where many other species gather and drink freely. Joining them are...

ADAM: Oh, wow. Let's see...a cheetah, gazelles, elephants, hyenas, and the Empire State Building. No, that doesn't sound right. Uh, a zebra. Yeah, that's better. Zebra. And a couple of hippos. Yeah, hippos. I really should write this down. *Whew*. This naming game is fast paced.

NARRATOR: The first man...

ADAM: Adam. You can call me Adam. That I *do* know. God called me that.

NARRATOR: ...is learning how to take care of the garden and tend to the animals. It's a challenging task.

ADAM: Oh, but I don't do it alone. Here's my beautiful wife. I call her Beatrice.

NARRATOR: Apparently Adam doesn't have this naming thing down quite yet. From the Garden of Eden, for the Animal Network, thank you for watching.

Get Real!

Check out Genesis 2:8-24 at the beginning of your Bible to see what really happened with God, Adam, Eve, and the garden. Believe it or not, God really did give Adam the responsibility of naming all the animal species. Whew, what a job!

2

What if a weather network reported on Noah's flood?

Early in the world's history, God got so sad about all the evil taking place that He decided to flood the whole earth and start over. But one man, whose name was Noah, loved God and always obeyed Him, so God gave him a way to keep people and the animals safe during the flood. God asked Noah to build a big boat so that Noah, his family, and two of every kind of animal could be rescued.

Noah obeyed the Lord and built the boat—and then it started raining. It rained for 40 days and 40 nights. Water even started gushing out from the inside the earth! The whole world was covered with water for more than a year, but Noah and his crew were safe and secure inside the ark.

What would this story sound like on a weather TV network?

TONYA THE WEATHER LADY: So once again, we'll have several dry days throughout the Great Plains and all the way to the coast. And that's your forecast. Now in our next story, what would you do if God gave you a special assignment—when you were 600 years old? And what might that assignment be? To give to the poor? To help

the elderly and orphans? But what if your assignment was to build a *yacht*? Well, our own Brad Cumulous is out in the field with a man who got that very assignment. Brad?

BRAD: Thanks, Tonya. A lot of people would say that boating is one of their favorite pastimes, but the man you're about to meet takes it a step further. Six-hundred-year-old Noah woke up one morning and heard a lot more than an alarm clock...

NOAH: As soon as I woke up that day, God spoke to me and told me He wanted to get a new start on planet Earth, so He was going to flood the whole thing. Well, I tell you, that kind of scared me. But then God said, "Noah, I've taken a liking to you. You're a good man who always follows Me, so I'll tell you what. If you build a big boat and take your family on board, you'll be saved."

"That's great, Lord," I said.

But then God added, "There is one small catch."

"What's that?" I asked.

"I need you to take two of every kind of animal in the world on board with you."

So that's what I did.

God told me exactly how big to make the boat and what kind of supplies to take on board. He's really thoughtful that way. So now all I have to do is wait for the rain.

BRAD: So tell me, Noah, how will you tell when the water has dried up? Are you going to tune in to our channel for updates? We're 24/7, you know."

NOAH: Actually, Brad, I think I'll just let a dove out the window. When she comes back with an olive branch in her mouth, I'll know the tops of the trees are showing above the water and things are drying up.

BRAD: Dove, trees...interesting.

BRAD: Well, as you can see, Tonya, Noah is keeping up his end of the bargain. He's got just about every type of animal on the...what do you call it? A ship? A boat?

NOAH: I call it an ark.

BRAD: Okay. Well, Tonya, what do you think? Is there rain in Noah's forecast?

TONYA: I'll say, Brad. Let's take a look at the satellite pictures. You can see we've got a low ridge coming in over the Euphrates Valley that's going to bring a storm front into the Babel basin. And it looks like it's going to be a doozey, with thunderstorms expected for the next several days. A storm watch has been issued for the area as well as a small craft advisory for the entire region.

Now, looking at the extended forecast...we can expect these conditions for the next 40 days and 40 nights.

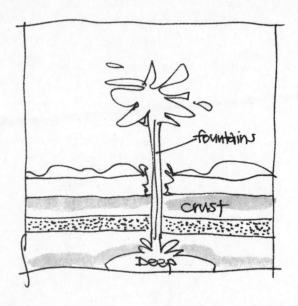

And Brad, here's something you don't see every day. Apparently the fountains of the deep are going to break up, bringing flooding to the outlying areas. Now, viewers, let's take a look at the weather where you live...

ANNOUNCER: Expect rain showers for an extended period with temperatures in the mid fifties to lower sixties and flooding to continue throughout the week.

TONYA: So if I were you, Brad, I'd get on that boat with Noah and the animals, where you can stay afloat.

BRAD: I'm way ahead of you, Tonya. It looks like the big door on the ark is closing, and we're off on our sea adventure. From the region of Ur of the Chaldeans, this is Brad Cumulous reporting for the Weather Network.

Get Real!

Noah's amazing story is recorded in Genesis 6–8. Grab your rain gear and check it out! Noah, his family, and the animals spent more than a year inside the ark before they came out and started a new life on earth. What would it have been like to be the only family on earth?

3

What if the Tower of Babel appeared in a movie preview?

After the flood, people and animals began to fill the earth again, and everyone spoke the same language. People could chat with each other—anywhere. But in the area that would later be called Babel, a whole bunch of folks got together to build a tower all the way to heaven. Of course, building a tall tower isn't a bad thing, but these people wanted to make themselves equal with God—and that's never a good idea. So to baffle the people of Babel, God confused their language so they couldn't understand each other. He also scattered them throughout the earth. But what if a movie preview told the story of the Tower of Babel? It might look like this...

DEEP, DRAMATIC VOICE: In a world where everyone speaks the same language, where people are out to make a name for themselves, and where everyone apparently had a little too much time on his hands, one man dares to stand up and speak out...

LEADER: I have an idea.
We need to build a tower!

CROWD: Hooray!

VOICE: He leads them with guts and courage.

LEADER: Come on, everyone!

CROWD: He's got guts—and courage!

VOICE: People from the entire region gather around.

LEADER: I need the Chaldeans over here, Assyrians over there!

VOICE: The plans are put in motion, and everything is right on schedule.

LEADER: Don't you see? With all of us working together nothing can stop us!

VOICE: But then...

INSPECTOR: I just got back from inspecting the tower. And it doesn't look good. Those trusses aren't up to code. If they're stressed at all, they'll never hold.

CROWD: We can't stop now; we're too far along!

VOICE: Then the unthinkble happens...

FIRST WORKER: It's the trusses—they're being stressed!

INSPECTOR: It's gonna blow! Everybody run!

LEADER: No, we've got to keep building! Just make it a little bit higher!

VOICE: Confusion spreads through the crowd...

SECOND WORKER: *No habla inglés!*

LEADER: What? I can't understand you!

INSPECTOR: Don't you see? Our languages have been confused. It's almost as if...(The crowd looks up.)

THIRD WORKER: *Sprechen zie Deutsch?*

(Credits roll…)

THE TOWER

A Robert D. Builder Film
A Higher and Higher Production

Starring Terrance Tower
Sylvia Bricksanmorter. Rock Boulder

Casting by Darlene Granite and Manny Tarr
Music by Marilyn Marble

Cinematography by Jamison Bricklayer BSB
(Babel Society of Builders)

Edited by Crane Hydraulics
Special Effects by Morrison Tectonic

Makeup by Cassandra Plaster
Art Director—Peter Sandstone

Key Grip—Tennyson Lathe
Best Boy—Edmund Piledriver

Written by Ken U. Diggitt
Produced by Sibyl Engineering

Directed by Robert D. Builder

Opens Friday nationwide
Rated I for Immature

Get Real!

If you missed the movie, check out the story in Genesis 11:1-9.

4

What if Abraham and Sarah drove to Canaan?

Abraham was the very first in a line of people that God would call His chosen ones. But in order to start this new group of people, God needed Abraham and his wife to move into the land God wanted to give to them. So God spoke to Abraham and told him to leave his hometown and go wherever He said to go. Of course, in those days, people traveled on foot, and the journey could take months or even years. But what if Abraham and Sarah drove an SUV? They'd pack it up, buy some snacks, and hit the road...

Abraham loaded the last of the suitcases onto the top of the SUV and then stretched. "Let's go—we want to make the oasis by sundown!" he shouted toward the house where his wife, Sarah, and his nephew, Lot, grabbed a few more belongings that might come in handy in this new place—wherever it was.

Out on the front lawn, Howard, the real estate agent, stood looking at the property as Sarah joined her husband by the SUV. "We're sure going to miss you two," he said with a sigh. "You are definitely the nicest eighty-year-old couple still hoping to have a baby we've ever had in this neighborhood."

Sarah laughed. "Oh, thanks so much," she said as she put the lunches in the SUV. "We're going to miss Haran too. But when Abraham says it's time to go, it's time to go."

Lot came down the front steps with the last two boxes of books and CDs. Abraham fastened the suitcases to the luggage racks with bungee cords.

"Where are you going again?" Howard asked.

"To a land that God will show us."

"Uh-huh," Howard said as he pulled the For Sale sign out of the ground. "Well, drive carefully and make sure you wear your seat belts."

As the trio headed up the on-ramp to Interstate 395, the Fertile Crescent Highway, Sarah turned to Abraham. "We *are* going to miss Haran. So much happened there." Abraham remembered the day his father first told them they were leaving the city of Ur and moving. Abraham had lived in Ur all his life until his whole family picked up and moved. They were supposed to go to a place called the Promised Land, but they ended up in Haran, a city near the Euphrates River. Abraham always knew they were supposed to keep going from there, but his dad just kind of settled down, and they never moved again. Until now.

Just a few days earlier, when God had spoken to Abraham and told him to move, Abraham was willing to obey God. But now, as he hit the gas pedal and stared ahead, he thought about how scary it was to not yet know where they were going. "Traffic's not too bad for a Friday," Abraham observed. He hated bumper-to-bumper traffic.

"Are we there yet?" Lot asked.

"No, not yet," Abraham answered. "God will let us know when we are."

"It looks like we're getting low on gas." Sarah said. "Maybe we should stop at the next station."

"Yeah," Lot added, "I wouldn't mind getting something to eat."

"We're almost to Shechem," Abraham said as he saw the sign indicating gas, food, and lodging ahead. "We can stop there."

Abraham pulled the van into the Shechem Gas-N-Go Easy Fuel gas station off exit 41578. He and Sarah got out and stretched. They looked at one another and smiled. Lot got out and headed for the convenience store.

"Ah, snacks for the journey," he said as he loaded his arms with chips, salsa, double chocolate sandwich cookies, mini-donuts, assorted nuts, jerky, and a couple of energy drinks. As he laid his purchase on the counter, the cashier looked up from her magazine.

"Just passing through?" she said.

"Yeah, kind of like a road trip," Lot said, adding a pack of gum to his purchase.

"Where you headed, hon?" she asked.

"To a land God will show us," Lot said.

"Uh-huh," she answered "That'll be eight seventy-nine."

They all got back into the car and took off. Lot ate his chips, mini-donuts, and one energy drink and then fell asleep with crumbs all over his T-shirt.

"How will we know when we get there?" Sarah asked as she looked out the window at the barren desert all around them.

"I think God will tell us. He's always led us in the past," Abraham said as he reached for the radio. "You never can get anything on the radio way out here, and unfortunately, all the CDs are packed."

"Yeah, we'll just have to travel in silence," Sarah said.

Off in the distance, she could see two little cities. She looked at her tour book. "Oh, those must be the twin cities, Sodom and Gomorrah. I think I've heard some rumors about them."

"Doesn't sound familiar," Abraham said as he moved the radio dial up and down. All he heard was static.

After another hour, Abraham pulled the SUV into the little settlement of Bethel. Lot opened his eyes and stretched. "Are we there yet?" he asked as he yawned.

"I think so," Abraham said. "We can stay here as long as the food holds out."

Sarah looked around. Could this possibly be the land that God was leading them to? "Come on, boys, help me unload the cooler with the sandwiches and soft drinks. And Lot, give me a hand with the hibachi. It looks like we might be here awhile."

Get Real!

Did Abraham, Sarah, and Lot ever make it to where they were supposed to go? Get out your Bible, look at Genesis 12:1-9, and check their itinerary.

5

What if Jacob and Esau were in a sitcom?

Jacob and Esau were twin brothers, the sons of Isaac, Abraham's son. Even though Esau was born first, they struggled with each other throughout their lives for first place in their family. One time, when Isaac was so old that he couldn't see, Jacob and his mom tricked Isaac into giving Jacob the special blessing of the firstborn. It had been intended for Esau.

The blessing of the firstborn was extremely important and meant special honor for the oldest son as well as a larger share of the inheritance. So Jacob put on Esau's clothes and even stuck lamb's wool on his arms and neck so he'd be as hairy as his brother. Then Jacob went to Isaac and pretended to be Esau.

The trick worked! But it threw Isaac's family into turmoil, and Jacob ended up running for his life. But what if this incident was replayed as a scene from a television sitcom, complete with a live studio audience? Would things have turned out differently?

ISAAC (Enters his family room from outside): Rebekah, have you seen my glasses? I want to bless the boys, but without my specs, I can't tell Jacob from Esau.

AUDIENCE: Ha ha ha.

REBEKAH: No, haven't seen them. Did you check out on the patio? (He leaves. Rebekah turns toward a bedroom and calls out in a whisper...) Jacob, quick! Come in here. Come on, don't be so shy. (Jacob enters from bedroom, dressed head to toe in lamb's wool.)

AUDIENCE: Ha ha ha ha ha.

JACOB: I feel ridiculous.

REBEKAH: You look great.

JACOB: Great? I look like a mattress that blew up at the factory!

AUDIENCE: Ha ha ha ha ha.

REBEKAH: Shhh! It's the only way we're gonna convince your father to give you Esau's blessing.

JACOB: What's the big deal about a blessing anyway? Is it really worth me going through all this?

REBEKAH: Are you kidding? It's the blessing of the firstborn.

JACOB: Firstborn? You've got to be kidding! Esau was born thirty seconds before me—it takes longer to make microwave popcorn!

AUDIENCE: Ha ha ha ha ha.

REBEKAH: No, don't you see? When Isaac gives you the blessing of the firstborn, you'll receive special honor in the family and the community. You'll also receive a bigger share of the inheritance.

JACOB: Really? I get more stuff?

REBEKAH: Yes! And there's no way I'll let that knucklehead brother of yours and his foreign wives get the rewards of that blessing. Quiet—here comes your father. Now remember...just follow my lead, and you'll know what to do.

ISAAC: Rebekah? Esau, is that you? I can't see anything without my glasses. (Rebekah holds the glasses up and smiles mischievously toward the audience.)

AUDIENCE: Ha ha ha ha ha.

ISAAC: Is that you, Esau my son?

JACOB: Yeah. (Lowers voice) I mean, yeah. It's me, Esau.

ISAAC: Did you bring me some dinner?

JACOB: Oh. I, uh...(Rebekah brings food and hands it to Jacob) Uh, yeah, it's some kind of meat I just shot out in the field.

ISAAC: Why is it in plastic wrap?

JACOB: Uh...well, some of the beasts wear it out there to keep fresh. It's the big fad. They call it the wildlife preserve.

AUDIENCE: Ha ha ha ha ha.

ISAAC: Come closer, my son. Is that really you, Esau?

JACOB: Of course. Who else would it be?

ISAAC: You sound like Jacob, but you smell like...(Rebekah throws a bunch of slop on Jacob.)

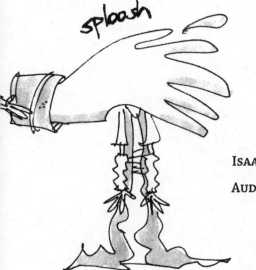

splaash

ISAAC: (winces)...Esau.

AUDIENCE: Ha ha ha ha ha.

ISAAC (moves over to lie down on the bed): Let me bless you, my son. (Jacob kneels.) May God bless you with His freshest dew, the abundance of the earth, and a continual supply of food. Let others serve you and nations bow down to you, and may you even rule over your brothers. Let no one succeed who curses you, and let anyone who blesses you be blessed.

JACOB: Amen.

JACOB (looking around): Well, thanks, Dad. Uh-oh, I think I hear Esau—I mean, Jacob coming. I better get out in the field again and continue my...whatever it is I do out there.

AUDIENCE: Ha ha ha ha ha.

ISAAC: Yes, my son. And thanks for the ribs and...what is this?

JACOB: A side of coleslaw?

AUDIENCE: Ha ha ha ha ha. (Applause.)

Get Real!

This is a crazy story, but it gets even crazier! Look at these passages in the Bible to see what happened between Jacob and Esau: Genesis 25:20-34; 27:1–28:5.

6

What if Joseph and his brothers were on a daytime talk show?

One of the most dramatic stories in the Old Testament is about a young man named Joseph and his 11 brothers. In a moment of extreme jealousy and hatred, his older brothers threw Joseph into a pit and left him there to die. Then they pulled him back out and sold him as a slave to some merchants passing by. The merchants went to Egypt and sold Joseph as a slave there. In Egypt, Joseph was blamed for a crime he didn't commit, and he was thrown into prison.

Joseph's situation sounds hopeless, doesn't it? But through God's miraculous workings, Joseph eventually became the king's second in command over the entire nation! Through all of this, Joseph learned to forgive his brothers and trust God in a new way. But what if Joseph and his brothers were featured on a daytime talk show—you know, the kind that encourages yelling and fighting? Would it end up like this?

MONTE SPANGLER: Hi, everybody, and welcome to *The Monte Spangler Show*, the show that puts the *fun* in dysfunctional! Well, today we're taking a look at young Egyptian rulers and the brothers who hate them. Live in our studio, please welcome the favorite son of Jacob, fancy coat and all, heeeeere's Joseph!

JOSEPH: Thank you.

MONTE: So, Joseph, you're called the favorite son of Jacob. What's that all about?

JOSEPH: I don't really like to talk about it anymore. It's caused all of us a lot of grief.

MONTE: Well, that's what we're here for—grief, anguish, fighting... that's what keeps our show so popular! And I must say, your family had it all.

JOSEPH: Yeah, Monte, that's right. You see, I started out living with my dad and brothers in the land of Canaan.

MONTE: Right. So how many boys are in your family?

JOSEPH: At the time there were 11 of us. Now there's 12. My brother Benjamin was born later.

MONTE: So go on. What about that coat of yours?

JOSEPH: Whoa, I almost forgot about that. How did you...

MONTE: Our researchers are thorough. And we pay big money for inside scoops. We dug up some great dirt on you, your family, and your wardrobe. So you had this special, fancy coat. And none of your brothers did, so I bet that made them pretty mad.

JOSEPH: Yeah. It was a coat of many colors, kind of like one a prince would wear.

MONTE: I bet that coat of many colors made them see *red* as they turned *green* with envy.

JOSEPH: You might say that.

MONTE: So how were things around the house? Or actually, out in the field?

JOSEPH: Not so good. In fact one day...

MONTE: I hate to interrupt you, Joey, but we had our hidden cameras on you that day when things went sour in the wilderness of Dothan. Let's take a look... Okay, there are your brothers...

———

SIMEON: Come on, Reuben, it's your turn to feed the flocks.

REUBEN: No it isn't, I did it last time. It's Judah's turn. I always have to do it!

LEVI: Hey, wait a second...here comes Joseph. Him and his big dreams.

JUDAH: Don't you just hate him sometimes?

REUBEN: Hey guys, check out this pit. Wouldn't it be a shame if Joseph fell in and we forgot about him and left him there?

LEVI: Hi, Joseph, what's up? Hey, come look at this pit. I think I dropped my hat down there. Can you see?

SIMEON: Throw him in!

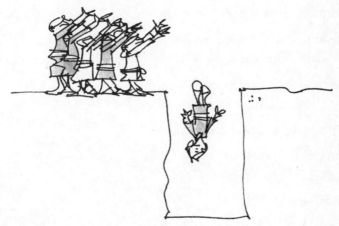

MONTE: Whoa, that must have been a traumatic experience for you, Joseph.

JOSEPH: Yeah, it was, Monte. But they didn't leave me in there too long.

MONTE: That was nice of them.

JOSEPH: Not really. They pulled me up and sold me as a slave to a bunch of Ishmaelite traders who just happened to come by.

MONTE: That made you really mad, didn't it, Joseph? So mad that all you could think about was revenge!

JOSEPH: Well, for a while, maybe...

MONTE: So what would happen if you saw those rotten brothers of yours face-to-face?

JOSEPH: Well...

MONTE: Hold onto your seat everybody! We've got those evil brothers backstage! Ha! Bring 'em on out!

JOSEPH: Are you serious?

MONTE: You bet! *Now* the fireworks are going to begin! I can't wait to hear the insults! The name calling! The big fat fight! Watch this, everybody, Joseph is getting up...he's going over to his brothers, and I'll bet he's going to give it to them. In fact, he's—wait a minute, he's hugging them! What? That's not supposed to happen! Stop that! Stop hugging! We need some conflict here. What are you doing? I wanted fireworks! I want conflict, rage, revenge!

JOSEPH: Well, Monte, if you'd let me explain...I've already seen my brothers and forgiven them. After they sent me to Egypt, I became the head servant at the house of one of Pharaoh's captains. And after I spent about 13 years as a slave and then in prison for a crime I didn't commit, God actually got me out and put me in charge of all of Egypt. While I was overseeing the country's supplies, there was a huge famine, and all of Egypt came to me for food. My brothers even came down from Canaan to get food.

REUBEN: But we didn't realize it was Joseph.

SIMEON: He looked really different.

MONTE: I just don't get it. How could you forgive your brothers after all they did to you?"

JOSEPH: To be honest, it wasn't easy. But then one day I realized that it wasn't my brothers who sent me to Egypt, it was God! And He had a plan for me and for all of Egypt and the rest of the world. In fact, if that hadn't happened, or if I hadn't forgiven my brothers, the entire nation of Israel could have disappeared completely.

MONTE: Well, this has never happened before. Forgiveness doesn't make good TV! Out! Out! Off my stage! (To audience) Thanks, everybody. We have a dynamite show lined up for tomorrow! We've got a king named Ahab, a prophet named Elijah, and Ahab's wife, Jezebel. Boy, we're gonna see some fireworks then! Don't miss it!

Get Real!

During his time as a slave and a prisoner, Joseph started to realize that God had a plan for him and his family all along. So Joseph forgave his brothers and even helped them to get food during the worldwide shortage. Because of Joseph's obedience and forgiveness, God saved his entire family from starvation. Read all about it in Genesis 37 and 39–48.

7

What if Moses had a GPS?

When Moses was 80 years old, God appeared to him and asked him to help rescue the Israelites from the harsh treatment they were enduring in Egypt. God told Moses that He was going to lead them all to a new land, where they would live in peace and prosperity. After a very long time pleading with Pharaoh, the ruler of Egypt, God's people were released. Now Moses had the huge job of leading almost two million people out of Egypt and 300 miles north to the Promised Land. It was a long journey that they hadn't taken before, but what if Moses used a GPS device to find his way? Would that have made their journey any easier?

Moses woke up early on this, the most special day of his entire life. Finally, after months of Moses' pleas, Pharaoh had agreed to let him lead God's people, the Israelites, out of Egypt and into the Promised Land.

Pharaoh took a long time to follow through on that agreement, so Moses started to doubt whether he had heard God's instructions right. But finally, after many months and ten plagues that were destroying Egypt, the stubborn ruler finally agreed to release God's people.

Moses looked in the mirror. In just a few minutes, he'd stand in front of almost two million people and lead them to freedom in the land that God had promised to them.

As he tightened the belt to his robe, a thought struck him. "Where *is* this place, and how am I going to get all of these people to follow me?" Moses started to feel nervous. Then he remembered that his family had given him a—what was it called? Global Positioning System?—last year for his seventy-ninth birthday. He'd never opened it because he didn't think he could understand it. Besides, what's a globe?

He rummaged around in the closet...where was it?

Moses' wife, Zipporah, yelled from the other room. "Everybody's waiting for us!"

There it was, still in the box. Moses pulled it out and looked at it. It had a screen and a couple of buttons. He looked around, pushed the green button, and watched in amazement as the screen lit up.

Suddenly a woman's voice came out of nowhere. "Say a command."

Moses jumped and almost dropped the device.

"Who's in there with you?" Zipporah asked from the other room. "Is that Aunt Sylvia?"

"No, it's just the GPS," Moses replied.

"Say a command," it demanded again. Moses spoke directly to the screen in a slow, loud voice, "Need directions."

Nothing happened for a second, but then the screen changed to bluish green. At the top of the screen, a line read, "Starting point." Moses slowly typed in "Bondage in Egypt." Right below that, another line appeared: "Destination." Moses looked around again, typed "Promised Land" as quickly as he could, and pushed the Enter button.

Just as he did, Zipporah appeared in the doorway with two suit-cases and her cosmetic bag. "What's that?" she asked.

Moses turned with a smile. "A GPS," he said. "It'll lead us to where we need to go. It's guaranteed."

"I thought God was going to lead us," she said as she put the kneading bowl into her bag.

"Well, I know He will..." Moses began, but he was interrupted by the GPS lady. "Directions are ready."

Zipporah jumped. "It talks to you?"

"Yeah, I think that'll make it easier," Moses said as he pushed the button to begin. "It's about to start..."

The GPS lit up. "Step 1: Walk to front door and open it."

"We knew that." Zipporah said as she rolled her eyes. "How much did we pay for that thing?" Nonetheless, she and Moses obediently followed. They walked to the front door and opened it.

"Turn left and walk to the end of the block. Twenty-six feet."

"We know that!" Zipporah said as she pulled her suitcases along.

"Walk twenty feet to Palm Avenue and turn right."

"This is going to take forever," Zipporah moaned.

Finally she and Moses reached a huge square on the edge of town where all the Israelites had gathered. All of them carried baskets or bags containing all their worldly possessions as well as the gold and silver that their Egyptian neighbors had given them. Some were in carts, but most were on foot.

Moses stood up on the foundation of a sphinx and addressed the crowd.

"Today is a day of great deliverance. Our God has freed us from the slavery we've experienced for four hundred years here in Egypt. Follow me as I follow God, and He will take us to the Promised Land!" Everyone shouted, sang, and praised God. Moses prayed for everyone and then turned to check the tiny screen on the GPS.

Moses pressed the Directions button again, and the screen lit up. "Head north through land of Philistines to Promised Land. Turn left at Jordan River. 250 miles."

"I hate that thing already," Zipporah said to a lady on her left who was managing three kids.

"Well," Moses said, looking north, "according to this, we should be there in about three weeks. Here we go!"

But something strange happened as they left Egypt. God told Moses to turn right and head toward the Red Sea. Moses stopped and looked around. The GPS directed them to keep going straight— the most direct route to the Promised Land.

"This can't be right," Moses said as he shook the GPS. "Maybe this thing is a little off. Let's go right."

"Just as God says," Zipporah added. So they traveled east for several days.

Moses was getting sleepy as he and his two million friends trudged through the desert. But suddenly the GPS came to life—"Wrong turn! Make U-turn immediately!"

Moses looked at the gadget and then looked up just in time to see water! It was the Red Sea—right in their path!

"Isn't this the way God told us to go?" he thought. "This can't be right! Why would God lead us to a dead end?" Moses stopped suddenly, and his two million companions bumped into each other.

"What are we doing here?" a middle-aged man asked.

"This can't be right! Why didn't you follow the GPS?" the man's wife added.

"Well," Moses answered, "the GPS said Go Straight, but God led us here to the edge of the Red Sea, so I just sort of followed God."

"But how are we going to get across?" they all yelled.

"Well, I guess we'll just have to trust God."

And sure enough, the next day God provided the first of many miracles He performed on the desert journey. Just as Pharaoh's army closed in on Moses and the people, God opened up the Red Sea, and all the Israelites walked through on dry land! And somewhere in the midst of the sea, rumor has it that Moses lost the GPS unit once and for all. It's probably just as well because Moses and all the people followed God the rest of the way to the Promised Land.

Get Real!

Well, instead of three weeks, the trip from Egypt to the Promised Land took more than 40 years! That's because the Israelites had to learn some lessons of obedience and warfare before they were able to enter the land God had prepared for them.

But the good news is that Moses and God's people didn't need a GPS—they had God's leading every single day they were in the desert. He led them by a pillar of cloud during the day and a pillar of fire by night. These signs not only guided them but also provided extra help and comfort for the journey. The cloud gave them shade and protection during the day, and the fire gave them light and warmth all night. Those 40 years of wandering in the desert taught the people that following and obeying God is the only way to get where you need to go.

8

What if a commercial advertised a product called Manna?

God never left Moses and His people during their years of wandering in the wilderness. He also kept His promise to feed them and take care of them. Every morning when the Israelites woke up, they found a delicious food on the ground. It was called *manna* (which actually means, "What is it?"). It looked like white coriander seeds and tasted like honey wafers, and it gave them all the nutrition they needed for that day. God told the people to gather the manna every day. If they tried to stockpile the manna or keep it longer than one day, it became moldy and stinky.

The manna was a sign of God's daily care and provision, and God wanted all the people to learn to trust Him day by day. It was the Israelites' daily miracle.

But what if someone decided to make a commercial for Manna? Would it look like this?

ANNOUNCER: Moms, how often do you hear this familiar question?

KID: Hey Mom, what's for dinner?

MOM: Between washing, raising the kids, and wandering through the desert, who has time to come up with a tasty, nutritious meal? I'm at my wit's end!

ANNOUNCER: Well don't worry, Mom, your troubles are over!

Introducing Manna, the delicious, easy, and fascinating meal packed with everything your family needs for the day.

DAD: It has that appealing white coriander-seed look.

KID: I love it because it tastes like wafers made of honey.

MOM: And I trust Manna because I know my family's getting the vitamins and minerals they need for those long days and cold nights in the Sinai Peninsula.

ALL: And twice as much on Friday!

MOM: Plus, every package of manna comes with its very own freshness date.

Why look, we need to eat this today!

ANNOUNCER: So enjoy Manna today and every day.

And when your family asks "What's the manna?" you can say "All is well because we have a daily gift from God."

(**ANNOUNCER CONTINUES BUT MUCH FASTER**): Not available outside the desert. Manna must be eaten by freshness date or it will breed worms and stink. Gather what you need daily. Some restrictions apply.

Get Real!

The manna fed and nourished the Israelites for 40 years in the wilderness, but the main reason God gave it to them was to remind them to trust and rely on Him daily to take care of their needs. That's a lesson we all can learn. Read the whole story in Exodus 16.

9

What if Joshua's battle at Jericho inspired a video game?

After the Israelites had wandered in the desert for 40 years and Moses had died, God chose Joshua to be their new general and to take the people into the Promised Land (which includes modern-day Israel). Their first task was to take over Jericho, a strong city surrounded by huge walls.

Weeks before the battle, Joshua sent two spies into the city to scout it out. While they were there, they met a young woman named Rahab. She helped the spies and even hid them from danger. As the two spies left Rahab's house, she said, "I know that God has given this city into your hands. Remember me and spare me when you attack."

The spies agreed and told her to hang a scarlet rope from her window to help them identify her house when the battle took place.

Meanwhile, God's strategic plan for taking the city of Jericho was to have the people march around the city silently once a day for six days. On the seventh day they were to march around it seven times and then give a loud shout and blow trumpets. God promised that when they did, the protective walls would fall down, and victory would be theirs.

But what if Joshua, Rahab, the spies, and the whole battle were part of a video game? Do you think the Israelites would be able to find Rahab in all the confusion and get her out in time?

Resume Game

New Game

One Player

Two Players

Two Million Players

JERICHO IV
Black Ops

Mission Objectives

Perform reconnaissance of Jericho: Accomplished

Perform reconnaissance of Rahab's house: Accomplished

Extract Rahab and family: In progress

Take the city: In progress

Proceed to level 2

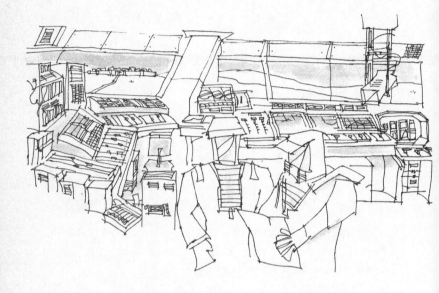

0600 HOURS—JOSHUA'S CAMP OUTSIDE GILGAL

"All right, you guys, get over here."

"Yeah? What is it, Josh? Oh, sorry—I mean, Captain."

"God told us to hit Jericho. In about an hour we're going in."

"So how are we going to do it? Firepower? Air assault? Penetrate the perimeter and take out the wall?"

"None of the above. I've got a brilliant plan. They'll never expect it."

"No offense, Captain, but we've all felt kind of silly walking around the city for the last six days saying nothing."

"I did that on purpose. After hearing you all grumble for that past 40 years, I thought it might be a good idea to keep silent."

"Don't tell me—we're gonna walk around the city one more time, right?"

"Nope."

"Good."

"We're gonna walk around it seven times. Then I'll have the priests blow the trumpets, and we'll shout as loud as we can. That's when the fun starts."

"Roger that."

"Loomis? Powers? I want you two to get in, go through the back alleys, get to Rahab's house, and get her family out. No looking around, no taking stuff, no nothing. You got it?"

"Got it. Captain? How are we gonna find her? It'll be crazy in there."

"Intel told us she'll hang a scarlet cord outside her window. That way you can spot the house, get in, extract the family, and get out before the enemy knows we've even been there."

"Good. Let's go!"

0800 HOURS—OUTSIDE JERICHO

Powers is thinking, "I'm getting tired of walking. How many times has it been? Six or seven. Wait—listen! There's the trumpet!"

"Everybody shout!"

"The walls are falling!"

"Okay! I'm goin' in!"

"Over here—follow me down this alley."

"Look out! Behind you! Look—it's the scarlet cord!"

"Lay down some cover for me. I'll get the family!"

"Rahab! It's Sergeant Loomis and Lieutenant Powers! We've been sent to extract you!"

"What's happening?"

"Come with us...Let's go out this way. Company B is keeping them busy on the other side."

"We got them!"

SUCCESSFUL EXTRACTION—20,000 POINTS

"This was a piece of cake. The next city on our map is a little place called Ai. Hmmm. How hard can that be?"

Get Real!

This is a cool story of courage, victory, and trusting God. Read the whole thing in Joshua 2 and Joshua 6.

10

What if CSI agents investigated Achan's theft?

When God told Joshua how to defeat Jericho, He also commanded that no one steal anything from the city. All of the goods were to be given to God as a sign of the people's trust and obedience. In this little-known story from the book of Joshua in the Old Testament, an Israelite named Achan disobeyed God's command. He gave in to temptation and stole some valuable items from a house in Jericho. As a result of Achan's secret disobedience, the Israelites couldn't move on.

At first, Joshua could not figure out what had happened. Then God showed Joshua who the guilty party was, and Achan and his family were punished. But what if Joshua had called in some crime scene investigators to solve the mystery instead?

CSI HEADQUARTERS, 1:47 P.M.

Joshua and Achan sat in interrogation room one. They looked dazed, confused. Something was out of balance, and Joshua didn't seem to be able to figure out what it was. Cutter and I had been assigned to the case.

Achan was the first to speak. He was short with a dark goatee. Something about him didn't seem right.

"It was unbelievable," he said. "The whole wall fell down. We didn't have to do a thing."

Then Joshua spoke up. "But something was wrong. I just knew that something had been stolen."

"No way!" Achan said.

"What's the big deal with that?" Cutter asked. "Don't people always take stuff during a battle? I mean, I thought that was the point—the spoils of victory."

"Yeah, plunder," Joshua said. "You always get to take the stuff you won. But that's just it…"

"What?" Cutter asked.

"God told us not to take any loot," Joshua said. "Not this time. All of this—the people, the place, the gold, the cattle, the appliances—it was all supposed to be His. We weren't supposed to take anything for ourselves. So when we tried to fight against Ai, the next city on the list, we got thumped. They totally whipped us! That's when I knew something was up."

We could see this was going nowhere, so we let the two of them go. As they walked down the hall, Cutter commented to Achan on the beautiful purple robe he was wearing.

"Nice garment."

"Thanks. It's Babylonian."

He disappeared out the side door, and Cutter looked at me.

"What do you think?" Cutter said. "Think Joshua's telling the truth?"

"Yeah, he's got no reason to lie. Besides, they're pretty much stuck."

"Stuck?"

"Yeah, they can't go on in their conquest until this thing gets ironed out."

Cutter looked at me, and we were both thinking the same thing. Time to head out to the crime scene.

JERICHO, 3:48 P.M.

We arrived at what had been the bustling city of Jericho. There was nothing left. It was just as they'd told us. The entire wall had fallen down flat.

A uniformed officer walked up.

"Did you find anything on the surveillance cameras?" I asked.

"Nothin'."

"Why is that?"

"Surveillance cameras won't be invented for more than three thousand years."

"Good point."

Cutter spotted something on the ground next to what was once a house. He bent down and picked up a shiny object. "Hey, take a look at this," he said. "We'd better get this to the lab."

CRIME LAB, 6:15 P.M.

Two hours later, the lab results confirmed what we suspected.

Dr. Hildebrand said, "Look at this through the microscope. It's just dust, but it's one hundred percent AU."

"AU?"

"Gold. And it's pure. Oh, and Cutter? There was something else."

"What?"

"I also found a thread."

"Yeah?"

"It's from a Babylonian garment."

Cutter looked at me. It was time to close in.

THE ISRAELITE CAMP, 9:14 A.M.

By the time we got to the camp, Joshua had devised a plan to catch the culprit. Besides, God had told him He'd point out the guilty party. Joshua had gathered all the tribes together, and one by one, God had dismissed all but one.

It was Achan's tribe. We had a line-up. It was him.

"Mind if we have a word with you, Achan?"

"Sure. What's going on?" He looked around nervously.

"We'd like to take a look around your tent."

"You got a warrant?"

"Let's just say God told us we got probable cause. Bring it in, Cutter," I said, looking straight at Achan.

"What's that?" Achan asked. He was starting to sweat.

"It's called a SpectraScope. It picks up hair, fibers, DNA...If there's something in here that doesn't belong, we'll find it with this. This thing is so precise it'll even tell us what you had for lunch."

"You got nothin' on me."

"Then you probably won't mind us looking around."

It didn't take long. The SpectraScope lit up and started beeping. There it was, right under a throw rug in the middle of Achan's tent. Two hundred shekels of silver, a wedge of gold, and—what do you know? A Babylonian garment.

Two uniforms appeared behind Achan and pulled out the hand-cuffs.

"Take him away." The SpectraScope never lies.

"By the way, Achan..."

"Yeah?"

"You had a pastrami and pickle sandwich and a diet soda."

"Huh?"

"For lunch. The SpectraScope told us."

I looked at Cutter. He smiled and turned to Joshua. "So what are you waiting for?" Cutter asked. "Don't you have some orders from the Top?"

Joshua nodded and turned to his lieutenants. "Muster the troops, it's time to take Ai!"

Mystery solved. Mission accomplished.

Get Real!

Achan's greed got him into trouble. It made him impatient and unwilling to trust in God's direction. If he had simply obeyed God, he would have been blessed, for when the people went to fight against the next city, God let them take anything they wanted (Joshua 8:1-2). You can read all about Joshua and Achan in Joshua 7.

11

What if Gideon competed on a game show?

During Israel's early history, in a time called the period of the Judges, enemies from all around Israel were constantly harassing God's people. One of the worst of these was a group called the Midianites, Israel's neighbors to the south. God recruited a man named Gideon to lead Israel in a battle against them.

But Gideon needed to learn how to trust and obey God. His first assignment was to go to his father's yard and pull down an idolatrous statue of a false god. When God gave him a second and larger assignment—to lead Israel against the Midianites—Gideon devised a test to make sure God was speaking to him. He put a piece of wool out on the ground overnight and asked God to make it wet with dew but to keep the ground dry. When that happened, he tried it again the next night, but this time he asked that the wool would be dry and the ground would be wet. When that happened too, Gideon knew that God was calling him to fight the Midianites.

Then came the biggest test of all. After Gideon had gathered an army of 32,000 fighting men to help him, God sent most of them home, leaving Gideon only 300 men to fight the entire Midianite army! God did that so that Gideon would know that *God* had won the battle, not him. But how would the story play out if Gideon competed on a game show and he won an all-expenses-paid trip to fight the Midianites?

JOHNNY: Welcome to *Beat Those Midianites!* It's the only television game show where you can win fabulous prizes as you save your people from oppression! And now, here's your host, Sterling Engedi!

AUDIENCE: (Applause.)

STERLING: Thanks so much, Johnny Johnison, and welcome to the show. As you remember, our current champion, Gideon, has done pretty well for himself this week. So I think he's ready to face those bullies who keep ripping off Israel's food, property, and possessions. Ladies and gentlemen, let's welcome Gideon!

AUDIENCE: (Applause.)

STERLING: Well, welcome back, Gideon. Now, you've already accomplished your first task—you tore down the false idol in your father's backyard.

GIDEON: Yeah, I had a couple of friends help me. We did it at night.

STERLING: At night? Wonderful. And yesterday during the lightning round, your piece of wool came up dry, so you know you're headed in the right direction.

GIDEON: Yeah, that was an encouraging sign from God.

STERLING: I'll bet it was. Well, what do you think, audience? Is Gideon ready to go for the big prize?

AUDIENCE: (Applause.)

STERLING: In that case...Johnny, tell Gideon what he's got in store.

JOHNNY: It's a once in a lifetime battle against the Midianites!

AUDIENCE: (Applause.)

JOHNNY: Yes, you and the army of your choice will travel to the scenic and picturesque hill of Moreh for three days and two fabulous nights of unforgettable action as you set the Midianites to flight. Swordplay, yelling, screaming, and hand-to-hand combat are just some of the activities you'll enjoy as you *Beat Those Midianites!*

GIDEON: Wow.

STERLING: Yes indeed, did you hear that audience? Gideon just said, "Wow."

AUDIENCE: (Applause.)

STERLING: Gideon, if you'll just step over here and spin the big Wheel of Opposition, we'll see just how many Midianites you're going to be facing. Here he goes, folks!

GIDEON: Big money, big money!

STERLING: Actually, Gideon, there's no money. It's just an army.

GIDEON: Oh.

AUDIENCE: (Applause.)

STERLING: You've landed on "As numerous as locusts." What do you think, audience? I'd say that's quite a few. Locusts are big grasshoppers that travel in swarms—there's usually thousands of them. Sounds like Midian's army is going to be pretty big!

GIDEON: Yeah, I know.

STERLING: That's not so good.

GIDEON: Yeah.

STERLING: But Gideon, as you know, you can choose the army you will use to defeat the Midianites. We have three armies hidden behind those three big doors on our trading floor. Which door will it be, Gideon? Door number one, door number two, or door number three? Audience, help him out!

AUDIENCE: (Yelling out numbers.)

GIDEON: I think I'll take door number three, Sterling.

STERLING: Door number three! But first, let's see what's behind the doors you *didn't* take. Open 'em up! Oh, door number one would have given you 33,000 warriors. Boy, I bet *that* would have given you a little confidence, wouldn't it? Tough break, Gideon. And now, let's see what's behind door number two...10,000 warriors! Oh, that's a shame. You know, having 10,000 soldiers with you would also make you feel pretty unbeatable.

STERLING: But you chose door number three. So let's open it up and see the army you have chosen.

AUDIENCE (after seeing results): Ohhh.

STERLING: Oh my, it's just 300 men. That's not much when you're going up against an army as numerous as locusts. What do you think, audience? I'd say Gideon's going to need some kind of miracle to defeat the Midianite army, wouldn't you say?

AUDIENCE: Mm-hmm...

GIDEON: I know just who to ask...

STERLING: Thanks so much for being with us today, Gideon, and good luck with that battle. But we don't want you to go away empty-handed. We have some lovely gifts for you. Johnny, what's Gideon going to take with him?

GIDEON: I hope it's some swords or tanks or at least a bow and arrow.

JOHNNY: It's a lovely outdoor patio set!

AUDIENCE: (Applause.)

JOHNNY: Yes, on those hot Judean summer nights, you'll enjoy ice cold beverages in this lovely selection of stone pitchers. And to keep things bright on your patio during your outdoor entertaining, you'll enjoy a variety of bright decorative torches. And don't forget musical entertainment! You and your three hundred men can initiate and celebrate your victory with an assortment of quality trumpets. All courtesy of *Beat those Midianties*!

AUDIENCE: (Applause.)

GIDEON: What am I going to do with these?

STERLING: Oh, you'll think of something. Hey, we're just about out of time. Thanks again to Gideon and to our studio audience. From Johnny and all of us here, we'll see you next time on *Beat those Midianites!*

Get Real!

That was pretty crazy wasn't it? But in the real story, God was the one who shrunk Gideon's army down to 300. And what did Gideon do with all those pitchers, torches, and trumpets? He gave everything he'd won (just kidding!) to his men, who hid in the brush all around the Midianite camp. They waited until the middle of the night, and then on Gideon's signal, they all lit their torches, broke their pitchers, and blew the trumpets. This scared and confused the Midianites so much that they actually started fighting each other!

God gave Gideon and all of Israel victory once and for all! Check out the real story in Judges 6–8. It's amazing!

12

What if Samson substituted as your PE teacher?

Not long after Gideon defeated the Midianites, another enemy—the Philistines—started harassing the people of Israel. They were a real pain in the neck for God's people. So God decided to raise up another leader who would fight them single-handedly. This warrior was named Samson, and he was strong. One time he lifted up the entrance gates of a city and walked 20 miles with them on his back! Another time he fought 1000 warriors by himself—and won!

What was the secret of Samson's supernatural strength? It was his hair! No kidding—when Samson was young, his parents made a vow to God, and it included a promise that Samson would never cut his hair. Samson made a lot of mistakes in his life, but he really did try to follow God in the end. But what if you went to school one day and discovered you had a substitute PE teacher—Samson! Do you think you'd survive?

Fourth period, The History of Algebra in the Fourteenth Century. You look at the clock. Your most favorite class, lunch, ended an hour ago. But your second-most favorite class is coming up: PE. You can't wait to run around, throw a ball, and maybe even tackle someone. It doesn't get any better than that—especially at Duncan Hines Middle School, where you're a seventh grader.

Finally the bell rings, but not before Cynthia Gant reminds the teacher that he forgot to assign the homework. As you slip into the hallway, you see your best friend, Josh. He's got a big grin on his face. "Did you hear? Coach Rorschach is gone today to wrestling finals. We've got a sub in PE."

"Cool!" You head to the locker room, where you swap your jeans and sweatshirt for your blue gym shorts and white T-shirt.

Josh makes a face as you put it on. "Whew," he asks, "When's the last time you washed that thing?"

"I'm supposed to wash it?"

Suddenly the locker room darkens. What is it? A power failure? An eclipse? No, something is blocking the light...

You look up at the biggest guy you've ever seen. He's, like, six feet eight, and he's got to weigh at least 390 pounds. And has, like, .02 percent body fat. One of his legs is slightly larger than Josh.

"Wh...wh...who are you?" you manage to get out.

"I'm your worst nightmare," he answers with a slight Austrian accent.

Josh lets out a little scream. Some of the other boys start crying.

You finish dressing and scurry out onto the field. When you get close, you realize this guy's got everybody standing in a straight line at rigid attention. Coach Rorschach never does that. The new guy slowly paces back and forth in front of the group. Almost all of the kids are shaking.

"My name is Samson. I'm your teacher today, and let me warn you, I'm not like any teacher you've ever had. I'm mean, tough, and stubborn, and I hold a grudge, so you don't want to make me mad."

Josh slowly raises his hand. "Mr. Samson?"

Samson snaps his head around and leans down to within a couple inches of Josh's face. Josh can smell what this guy had for breakfast, and it wasn't pretty. "Not *Mr.* Samson, just Samson. You got that, mister?"

Josh nods slightly. Little beads of sweat are forming on his forehead. Samson moves in closer. "Now, what was your question?"

"I forgot," Josh whispers. His eyes are as wide as your aunt Karen's dinner plates. Josh looks over at you, his eyes pleading, "Help me." You look back at him and shrug, as if to say, "You're on your own."

Samson stands up straight. All the kids follow his lead in fear and fascination. "Okay, we're gonna do some stretches. Everybody down! Give me 500 push-ups!"

"What happened to the stretches?" somebody dares to ask.

"These *are* the stretches!" he barks. "Wait till we get to the hard stuff!"

Peter Marpelwitz looks like he's going to be sick. Everybody drops to the grass. As Samson turns, you notice his hair. It's not just long, it's *girl* long—it goes all the way down to his waist. Whoa, there's got to be a story there. You remember your old history teacher who could easily be sidetracked if you got him talking about some other topic. Sometimes he'd talk the entire class and forget about schoolwork or homework. Deciding to take a chance, you look at Josh and say, "Psst" as you watch his awkward push-up position. His body forms a big *A*, and he doesn't go down all the way. He finally looks over at you.

"Watch" you whisper. You look up at Samson and ask in your most polite voice, "So how come your hair is so long?" You've done three of your 500 push-ups and are exhausted.

"Oh, that's a long story," he says.

"Tell us," you encourage innocently.

"Well, when I was born, my parents dedicated me to the Lord. They made a Nazarite vow, which means I can't drink alcohol and I can't touch dead things or dead people." He looks around at all of us. "It'd be a good vow for all of you to take!"

The whole class nods vigorously. No dead people. That seems like a good rule to you.

"Oh, and I'm not supposed to cut my hair. It's my hair that makes me so strong. Don't tell anyone though—it's a big secret. I won't even tell my girlfriend."

You look at your own arms and at Josh's. You both are shaking like blenders. You decide maybe you should grow your hair out.

"Okay, everybody up!" Samson barks. Everyone in the class struggles to his feet. You feel a little light-headed.

Josh is tracking with you. He whispers, "If we keep Samson talking, maybe we'll survive this." Then he turns to Samson and asks, "So what's the most you've ever lifted?"

Samson looks up for a moment, thinking. "Once I was in a town called Gath. The Philistines surrounded the whole place and were waiting to ambush me in the morning. So in the middle of the night, I got up, went over to the gates of the city, lifted them up, and carried them all the way to Hebron. That was, like, twenty miles."

"Oooh," the guys all say. "Cool."

Peter shouts out, "With the doors, bolts, and crossbar, that must have weighed more than twelve hundred pounds!"

Samson smiles. "Yeah, probably."

He's on a roll. Your body begins to relax.

"Then one time, the Philistines surrounded me, and I grabbed a dead donkey's jawbone and used it like a club. I beat 'em all. Must have been a thousand of them."

"Cool," the kids all say.

"Yeah," Samson says as he looks off in the distance, remembering. "Those were good times."

You're thinking about his Nazarite vow and the fact that he touched a dead donkey. That seems like a violation, but you choose not to mention it.

Samson rubs his hands together and says, "Okay, we're gonna do a little jogging. Let's run over to Ashkelon Peak and back . On your mark, get set…"

Your mind starts to race before your feet do. Ashkelon Peak is 270 miles away. It's just this side of the state line! You have to act fast. "Tell us more about the Philistines!" you blurt out.

Samson pauses for a second. Your distracting questions just might be working. He looks over toward the peak and runs his hand through his hair. You hold your breath. "Oh, they're the worst," he starts. Everyone breathes a sigh of relief as Samson continues. "They've been a pain to the Israelites ever since they arrived from Crete. They kept creeping into our land—you know, taking over farms and pastureland. Sometimes they raided us and stole all our stuff. Sometimes it got so bad, we had to pay them to leave us alone."

You look over at Butch Patterson, the class bully. He looks down. Samson continues, "So God heard everybody's prayer, and I guess He sent me to take care of them."

"Kind of like *The Enforcer*," Josh says. His cheeks are starting to regain some of their color.

"Yeah, you could say that," Samson says with a smile. "But things didn't turn out so good. I made some dumb choices—didn't listen to my parents, got a little self-centered. But I know God still has some plans for me." He stands up a little straighter. "So listen up, boys, learn from my mistakes. Obey your parents and don't do dumb things." He looks at the watch on his massive wrist. "Okay, I guess we're out of time. Head into the showers. And you'd better all get wet!"

While the other kids take off as if they're running for their lives, Josh looks at you and smiles. "Whew," he whispers.

"Yeah," you say, "we made it." Just then you hear *the voice* behind you.

"You there, stay where you are." You turn around slowly. Your heart has somehow crept up into your throat. Samson looks even bigger than he was before.

"Yes, sir?"

Samson smiles. "I'm on to you—getting me to talk so I wouldn't make you do the workout. You know, I wasn't really going to make you run to Ashkelon Peak." He laughs and then motions for you to join the others. "One more thing," he says. "You might think about growing your hair out."

Get Real!

Even though God enabled Samson to do some amazing feats of strength, it took Samson his whole life to understand the importance of following God completely. But Samson finally got the idea in the end. His story is told in Judges 13–16.

13

What if a sports network broadcast David's contest with Goliath?

Years later, the Philistines were at it again. (You'd think they would have learned after Samson.) This time, they were trying to take over Israel's land. King Saul rallied his troops, and they went to stand up against the Philistines.

When both armies were facing off in a beautiful valley named Elah, one of the Philistines came up with an idea. "Why don't we just have two guys fight each other, one from each side, and whoever wins that fight wins the battle. The losers will be the winners' slaves."

This idea sounded pretty fair to everyone. But the Philistines had a secret weapon—a 9-foot-tall, 400-hundred-pound warrior named Goliath who had never lost a fight. He'd be their representative. But who was going to fight Goliath? Would it be King Saul? Maybe one of his bodyguards?

Nobody was jumping at the chance to fight the Philistine giant.

Then a teenage shepherd who was pretty good with a slingshot heard about the challenge. The kid's name was David, and he knew that no giant was a match for his God. So David went out to face Goliath on the battlefield. But what if a sports channel broadcast the battle between David and Goliath? How would it turn out?

KURT: We're enjoying a beautiful day in the Valley of Elah and expecting an exciting albeit quick contest between the current champions, the Philistines, and the underdog challengers, the Israelites. Welcome to *The Game of the Week*. I'm Kurt Frontline, and I'm joined by my friend and colleague Matt Tailback for what could be a lopsided battle between the older and more experienced warrior, Goliath, and the young rookie from the little town of Bethlehem, the shepherd boy named David.

MATT: That's right, Kurt. I'm not sure how this matchup was chosen as the game of the week—nobody's got much hope for the little shepherd boy to go the distance with Goliath. Look at him!

KURT: I think we all agree, Matt, especially when we consider some of the stats. Compare these guys in size alone. Goliath is somewhere near six cubits and a span. Now for those of you at home who don't normally use the ancient Hebrew measurement system, that's almost ten feet tall. And from the look of him, I'm guessing he's weighing in at about four hundred pounds. On the other side, I'm looking at the kid, David, and he's...well, a lot less than that. What do you think? Maybe five feet seven and a small a hundred twenty pounds. I sure wouldn't want to be in his sandals right now.

KURT: Let's go down to the field, where Christy Overtime is on Israel's sidelines. What's happening down there, Christy?

CHRISTY: Frankly, Kurt, everybody's a little upset on this side of the field. Goliath has evidently been out here trash-talking the Israelites twice a day for forty days. Regardless of how many of these things you've been through, that's got to get to you. We caught up with Coach Saul just a few minutes ago, and this is what he had to say...

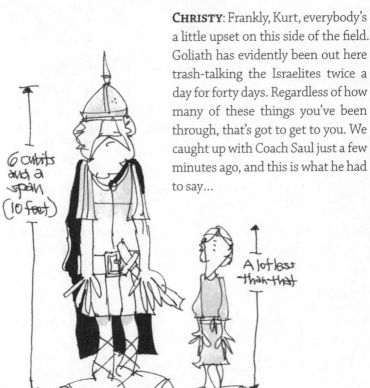

6 cubits and a span (10 feet)

A lot less ~~than that~~

CHRISTY: It's looking kind of scary out there, Coach—or rather, Your Highness. How did you prepare for today's contest?

COACH SAUL: I offered my armor to David, but the hardware didn't fit, and it was tripping him up. He decided to ditch the armor and go out there as is.

CHRISTY: Any last instructions for David?

COACH SAUL: No, I just told him to go out there and do his best. I also mentioned that his family has been notified.

CHRISTY: Thanks, Coach.

KURT: So Christy, can you describe the uniforms the players will be wearing today?

CHRISTY: That's an interesting point, Kurt. Once again, David seems to be outgunned. Goliath has the traditional red and black Philistine uniform that fans have grown to hate. The coat of mail around his midsection weighs a hundred twenty-six pounds, and he has bronze armor on his legs and a bronze javelin slung between his shoulders. We've seen all this before, but the Philistines are unveiling a new twist this season—a bronze helmet. You may recall that only the Philistines use bronze in their weapons, and that gives them a distinct advantage.

KURT: I hate to interrupt you, Christy, but Goliath appears to be moving out onto the field of play. Let's look at the view from the blimp. Even from up there he looks like an imposing figure out there in the sunlight. I can hardly see David.

KURT: Wait a minute—Goliath is saying something to David. Christy, can you make out what he's saying to the shepherd boy?

CHRISTY: Something about dogs and sticks and feeding David's body to the birds...you know, the regular stuff. And here we go—David is running *toward* the giant! What's that he's carrying, Matt?

MATT: I can't be sure, but from here it looks like a sling and five smooth stones. We've heard that David's tribe, Benjamin, is renowned for amazing accuracy with a slingshot.

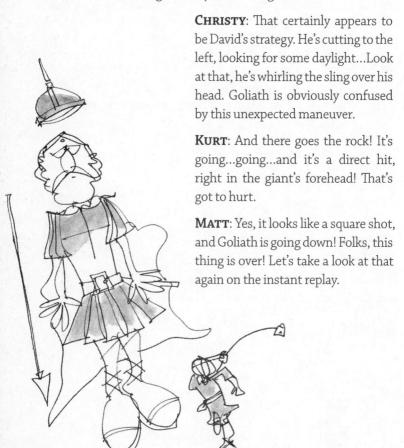

CHRISTY: That certainly appears to be David's strategy. He's cutting to the left, looking for some daylight...Look at that, he's whirling the sling over his head. Goliath is obviously confused by this unexpected maneuver.

KURT: And there goes the rock! It's going...going...and it's a direct hit, right in the giant's forehead! That's got to hurt.

MATT: Yes, it looks like a square shot, and Goliath is going down! Folks, this thing is over! Let's take a look at that again on the instant replay.

MATT: David's whirling the sling, and right...there! See how the rock comes out at just the right time? In slow motion you can see it's a perfect release, and there it goes. *Wham!* Now let's go back to the scene live down on the field.

KURT: And here we go. David's got Goliath's sword, and yes, it looks like he's about to cut off the giant's head. I don't think our viewers need to see that.

CHRISTY: Right you are, Kurt. This might be a good time to take a break and remind the fans that next week's contest is between the Warriors of Moab and the Mighty Army of Israel. All the action starts at six o'clock, nine o'clock Eastern, right here on ISPN—the Israel Sports and Programming Network. Until then, on behalf of our broadcast team, so long, and God bless you!

Get Real!

Tune in to the real play-by-play action of David's fight with Goliath in 1 Samuel 17. It really was a miracle from God that brought David victory that day.

14

What if a tabloid reported on David and Saul's troubles?

After David defeated Goliath, King Saul brought David into the palace to serve in the court and to act as one of the king's generals in battle. But soon, Saul became jealous of all the attention David was getting. The women of the kingdom even made up a song about Saul killing thousands but David killing *tens* of thousands. Ouch! That's hard on the ego!

Saul became so focused on getting even with David, he even threw a spear at him on more than one occasion. David fled from the palace and lived in the wilderness for years.

How would a tabloid magazine describe this situation? Magazines like that don't always get their facts straight, so as you read this story, try to determine how much is true and how much is made up as David and Saul go under the tabloid microscope.

HAIR TODAY, GONE TOMORROW

SAMSON AND DELILAH HAIR SALON SHOCKER!
Former hero back to beginner's gym

Jerusalem **FAKE TRUTH**
All the News ★ None of the Truth

SAUL TO DAVID: Get the Point?

Neighbors describe late-night spear throwing drama page 2

EXCLUSIVE
Boaz & Ruth's May-September Romance

JONAH SPEAKS OUT

"I'll never travel coach again!"

Israel, May 21. Professional jealousy is rocking the royal palace in Jerusalem. Rumors are flying since David, the former shepherd who has become something of a rock-star general, came on the scene a couple of months ago. Stories of jealousy, threats, and infighting have surfaced in the palace, creating a picture of royal life that's much different from the image portrayed in public.

"I've noticed a big change in the atmosphere around here," housekeeper Sylvia Burch commented under the condition of anonymity. "When David first moved in, it was kind of fun. You know, the new kid, the giant killer...it was really kind of exciting. He'd sit around and play his guitar or lyre or whatever it was and sing cool songs he'd written back when he was shepherd. And the music actually calmed King Saul. It was definitely quieter then."

Chef and counselor Aaron Shemp agreed. "We never see David anymore. Prince Jon said David was running for his life or some such thing. It's too bad; everybody really misses him. You're not going to print this, are you?"

Apparently, things were going well between the aging monarch and the young shepherd for several weeks after David killed Goliath. But according to sources in the palace, things turned sour in a hurry.

"My recollection is that it all got bad right after the ladies started singing that new song," reported Harold Nelson, an anonymous source close to the king. "You know, they'd sing, 'Saul has killed his thousands and David his *ten* thousands.' That really seemed to get under the king's skin. Looking back, I guess that might bug anybody."

On the surface, everything seems to be fine between Saul and David, as depicted in this photo of the two taken by the paparazzi at the opening of Zedekiah's Blacksmith and Weapons Shop in Jericho last month. But according to witnesses, the facade is hiding bad blood.

"Oh the blood is bad, it's very bad," said Claude Winslow, a landscaper and swan keeper on the palace grounds who asked to remain anonymous.

To further fuel those rumors, neighbors say that on Tuesday they heard a disturbance coming from the palace recital room. The ruckus allegedly included a spear-throwing incident. Saul reportedly got so mad at David, he actually hurled the eighteen pound weapon at the unarmed musician, missing him by inches. Even though neither party is commenting, we found a hole in the wall that Saul claims he created while trying to hang a picture.

David spoke through a representative last Friday. "Saul is God's chosen king of Israel, and I will continue to honor him."

Saul was not available for comment.

Get Real!

Saul's jealousy and suspicion of David started shortly after David's victory over Goliath and got worse over time. In fact, David had to spend years separated from his friends and family while he ran for his life from the angry king. You can read the entire account in 1 Samuel 18–31.

15

What if a home-improvement channel presented *Nehemiah's Extreme Makeover, Jerusalem Edition*?

Centuries after David reigned, the people of Israel forgot about God and stopped following Him. God sent the prophets to remind His people to obey Him, but these messengers were often ignored. As a result of Israel's unwillingness to listen to God, its cities were destroyed by the Babylonians, and the people were taken captive.

About 70 years later, God started bringing the Jews back to Israel. But when they returned, they couldn't believe what they saw. Their homeland looked like a wilderness. The capital city, Jerusalem, was in ruins—even the temple of God. Without walls to protect them, the people were in danger of attack from all sides. They felt hopeless and discouraged. So God brought a leader named Nehemiah to inspire everyone to rebuild the walls and live with hope again. Nehemiah divided the people into groups of families, and even though distractions and threats came from enemies all around, the people rebuilt the city wall in just a little more than six weeks!

But what if a TV show called *Nehemiah's Extreme Makeover, Jerusalem Edition* featured the rebuilding of the Jerusalem wall?

NEHEMIAH: Jerusalem has been called the city of God. It was a center of trade and commerce, a crossroads of the known world, and the worship center of the kingdom of Judah. That is, until 605 BC, when the Babylonians stormed into the area, creating an unbelievable path of destruction. When they were finished, the once impressive city of Jerusalem was reduced to a pile of rubble, and its people were taken captive. But that's all about to change—we're heading to that very region to help these people rebuilds their walls, their city, and their lives next on *Nehemiah's Extreme Makeover, Jerusalem Edition.*

NEHEMIAH (to team): We're on our way through the hills of Judah to the site that was once Israel's main capital. A few years ago, some Jewish captives in Babylon returned to Jerusalem. They wanted to rebuild, but financial pressures and discouragement from their enemies halted construction. In this region, a city needs walls for protection. Without walls, the residents are vulnerable to attack. So today we're going to help these people rebuild. Are you with me?

EXTREME TEAM: Leeeeeeet's do it!

—

NEHEMIAH: GOOD MORNING, GOD'S PEOPLE!

EXTREME TEAM: We're here to help you rebuild!

CROWD: Oh, this is unbelievable! This is wonderful!

NEHEMIAH: We spoke to some of the people who had recently moved back to Jerusalem.

JEWISH MOTHER: When we got back here with Ezra, our pastor, we couldn't believe our eyes. The place was uninhabitable. Everywhere we looked, we saw rubble and broken-down sections of wall...even the gates were burned. It was horrible. And we didn't even have running water.

JEWISH FATHER: We've *never* had that.

JEWISH MOTHER: But still...

NEHEMIAH: Normally we'd send you all somewhere on a big vacation, but frankly, we're going to need all of you to jump in and help rebuild your city. How do you feel about that?

CROWD: Hooray!

NEHEMIAH: That night I explored the walls, and everything I had heard was true. The place was in shambles. There were even some places we couldn't fit through. I had to bend down just to take a peek.

NEHEMIAH: The next morning, the whole community showed up ready to work. Our producers and I arranged the people into family groups and assigned them different sections to rebuild. For a complete list of everybody who helped, check out Nehemiah 3.

NEHEMIAH: The Extreme Team was amazed to see how fast everybody worked. After only a few weeks, the wall was halfway up. The only problems we had now were with some neighbors who weren't too happy about us rebuilding. There were a couple of grouches named Sanballat and Tobiah.

SANBALLAT: The whole thing is so stupid. What do they think they're doing? Do they really think they're going to get this wall rebuilt on time and on budget?

TOBIAH: It's so rickety that if even a fox jumped up on it, the whole thing would give way.

SANBALLAT: Good one, Tobiah!

NEHEMIAH: So when they threatened to attack us, I posted guards on the wall and encouraged the workers to wear their swords as they worked.

NEHEMIAH: Finally, after fifty-two days, the wall was complete! We invited everyone in the entire region to come get their first glimpse. And they'll see it right after this reminder...

———

ANNOUNCER: If you'd like to see more of the tools and weapons featured in tonight's episode, check out Nehemiah 4:13,16,21.

———

NEHEMIAH: Are you ready? All together now...

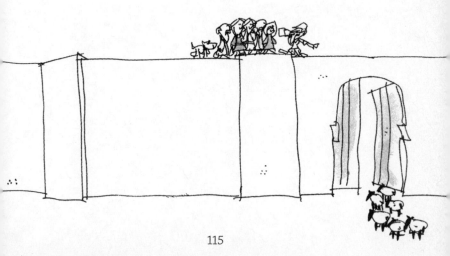

CROWD: MOVE THAT BUS! MOVE THAT BUS!

NEHEMIAH: Well, that's about it for Jerusalem. Next week we're going to be in the beautiful lakeside community of Capernaum to repair some roof damage at a small house. It seems some guys got really excited about seeing Jesus and cut a hole right in the middle of the roof in order to get their friend inside. Join us next week on *Nehemiah's Extreme Makeover, Jerusalem Edition*!

Get Real!

We have no idea what an amazing architectural feat it was to rebuild the wall in just 52 days, especially without all the tools that are available to us now. If you want to read more about Nehemiah and some other adventures he had, check out the book of Nehemiah in the Old Testament.

16

What if John the Baptist sat in as an early morning radio personality?

How do you get people ready for a visit from God? What do you tell them? God knew that the Jews needed some preparation before Jesus began His public ministry, so He decided to send a messenger in advance of Jesus. This messenger was named John the Baptist. John was an interesting choice. He was very committed to God, and he was a wild man! He lived by himself in the desert and wore a shirt made out of camel hide. And his diet was—get ready—grasshoppers and honey!

Yuk.

But John knew that his job was to introduce people to Jesus. And he didn't beat around the bush. He told the people to follow God, not just with their words but also in their actions. He wasn't even afraid to scold the hypocritical leaders of the time. His bold tell-it-like-it-is style got him in trouble more than once.

But what if John the Baptist sat in as an early morning radio personality, playing music, taking calls, and checking on traffic? Would he get his message out? And would his style earn him ratings and hearts for God?

"Goooood morrrrning, Jordan Valley! It's me, Mr. Intensity, your Voice of the Valley, John the Baptist, with today's news, weather, chariot race scores, and fifteen songs in a row right here on KWTR AM broadcasting, just outside the beautiful city of Jericho. It's fifteen minutes before the hour, and it's shaping up to be a beautiful day here in the Jordan wilderness—a perfect day to spend by the river. In fact, I'll baptize several lucky listeners later today, so keep listening for your chance to win.

"The forecast calls for partly cloudy conditions, with highs in the upper seventies. River levels are at twelve feet, and right now it's sixty-seven degrees and clear.

"Let's take a look at some of the famous people who are celebrating birthdays today. One of the three wise men is celebrating his fifty-eighth birthday. Quirinius, the governor of Syria, is 43 today. And over in Rome, Mrs. Caesar just turned 29. Again. Congratulations to all of you. Let's sing to them..."

"Okay, the phones are busy, so let's see what's happening out there this morning. Hello, this is John the Baptist on K-Water. Who's this?"

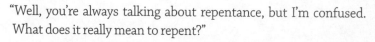

"This is Sophie."

"Hi, Sophie, how are you?"

"Just great, John. Love the show."

"Great, so what's on your mind?"

"Well, you're always talking about repentance, but I'm confused. What does it really mean to repent?"

"Good question. You know, everywhere I go—airports, coffee shops, taxis—people want to know what repentance means. Well, Sophie, repentance is simply changing your mind. It's like going one way but then realizing it's not good, so you turn around."

"So then your actions and behaviors...they would change too, right? They'd go in the new direction as well?"

"You got it, Sophie. So when I tell people to repent, it simply means to take a look at how they're living, and if they're doing something God would not be happy with, to make the change.

"Thanks so much— that's really helpful."

"You bet, Sophie—thanks for the call. Okay, next caller—who's this?"

"This is Allen from Upper Bethlehem."

"Beautiful country out there. What's on your mind?"

"I was just listening to your last caller, and I'd like to know, how can I tell whether I've really repented?"

"Another great question. I like to tell people they should see the changes in their lives. Are you treating people better? Are you being honest? Speaking the truth? Being kind?"

"I get what you mean—like bearing fruit worthy of repentance."

"You got it, man. Hey, we've got to take a break and hear from one of our fine sponsors, Lucky Jake's Jordan Desert Warehouse. You know, a camel-hair blazer and a matching belt really make a nice fashion statement whether you're headed for an important speaking engagement or just a nice evening out. Elsewhere you'd pay three hundred shekels for this sporty ensemble, but at Jake's Jordan Warehouse,

we're slashing prices so you can get the entire combination right off the rack for fifty-nine ninety-five. That's right, just fifty-nine ninety-five! Jake's Jordan Desert Warehouse—you'll walk out a new man.

"I also want to thank Manny's Deli for sending over these great snacks this morning. Mmmm, these are the best grasshoppers and honey I've ever tasted. Thanks, Manny, and keep up the good work!

"Okay, let's go out to our traffic reporter, Captain Maximilian Airborne, and see what's going on out there on the roads. What's happening, Max?"

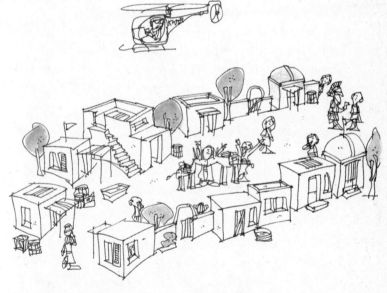

"Hey, John, the commute's not too bad out here this morning, even with a lot of people heading out for the weekend. We did have a little run-in at the corner of Solomon and Pomegranate. Two donkeys

121

appear to have run into each other. No injuries, but traffic is still a little slow in the area. And a couple of Roman soldiers have asked some civilians to carry their packs for a mile, so that's also causing some slowing. Other than that, things look pretty good out here. This is Captain Max for KWTR traffic."

"Thanks, Max. We'll keep an eye on that. We're almost at the top of the hour, so here's a quick message to the Pharisees and Sadducees out there listening: YOU BROOD OF SNAKES! YOU BETTER CHANGE YOUR WAYS, OR YOU'RE HEADING FOR BIG TROUBLE! Let's see your lives start lining up with your words. In other words, WALK THE TALK, you whitewashed tombs!

"Hey, it's almost nine o'clock, and you know what that means—coming up right after the break is the best personality on the air, anywhere. He's the reason you even *listen* to the radio. I'm happy to be His early morning warm-up guy. That's right, Jesus Himself is coming up right after me, and He is sooo much better than me. We're not even in the same league. I'm not worthy to tie His shoes, if you know what I mean, but I love going on the air before Him. So whatever you do, don't go away. He's coming up next, right here on KWTR, Jericho.

"But first, it's time to get back to the music. Here's a song from the Maccabean period called "Hold On!" And one more time, if you want to follow God, you've got to change your mind, your actions, and your attitude. This is Mr. Intensity, saying have a great day and stay tuned for the Real Man. And remember: Repent!"

Get Real!

God had a special assignment for John the Baptist. He was to announce to all Israel that God's Son was coming soon. And when Jesus came on the scene, John stepped back and let Jesus have the spotlight. John didn't need attention; he just wanted to please God. John is mentioned in all four of the Gospels—Matthew, Mark, Luke, and John.

17

What if Jesus texted the Beatitudes?

Everywhere Jesus went, huge crowds followed. Who was this guy? He knew God really well, He was kind and compassionate, and He was always helping people.

One afternoon, Jesus walked up a hillside and sat down. As usual, hundreds of people followed Him and gathered around to hear Him teach. He started to explain to them the way God's kingdom works here and in heaven. During this message, Jesus spoke what came to be known as the Beatitudes. They showed how things of the kingdom of God often seem backward from this world's perspective. For example, He said, "Happy are the meek—you know, the humble ones who let others go first—they'll inherit the whole world." How can that be? It seems like the movers and shakers inherit everything! Jesus had a whole list of these Beatitudes.

Jesus used the methods available to Him to share this good news with all the people on the hillside that day. But what if Jesus *texted* the Beatitudes to all His BFFs? (That's you and me.) See if you can interpret this modern-day version of His message. Then check out Matthew 5:2-12 to see how close you got.

SRMN ON TH MNT

☺ r th pr in sprt they gt th kngdm

☺ r th sad they'll b cmfrtd

☺ r th meek they gt th erth

☺ r thos who look 4 rightsness & peace they'll b filld

☺ r th mrcifl they gt mrcy

☺ r th pur in hrt they c God

☺ r th peacemkrs they r God's kids

☺ r th 1s pt dwn for good they 2 gt th kngdm

18

What if Zacchaeus ran a fast-food restaurant?

One of the coolest stories in the New Testament is about a short man named Zacchaeus. Besides having a funny name, this guy was really unpopular. He was a tax collector for the Roman government. And if that wasn't bad enough, he also ripped off people. He'd charge them more than Rome required, and he'd keep the extra money for himself. As you can imagine, nobody liked this guy at all. Who could blame them?

One day, Jesus came to Jericho, the town where Zacchaeus lived, and a huge crowd came out to see Him. Zacchaeus wasn't tall enough to see above the crowd, and he didn't have any friends to help him out. So he ran ahead of Jesus, climbed up a tree, and watched the whole procession from up above. He thought no one would notice, but when Jesus walked by the tree where Zacchaeus was perched, He stopped the parade and looked straight up at him. Jesus called Zacchaeus by name and said, "I want to come over to your house for lunch." Zacchaeus almost fell off the limb!

Jesus and the man that nobody loved had lunch together. When Zacchaeus felt Jesus' love and acceptance, his whole life changed. He became honest! And generous! He even gave back what he had taken. But what if Zacchaeus owned a fast-food restaurant? Would you get your money's worth? Would he overcharge you? And would you like fries with that?

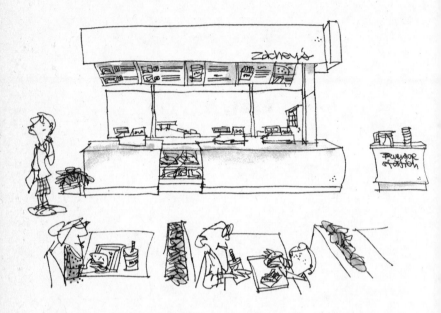

"Oh boy, I sure am hungry," you think as you open the door to your favorite fast-food place. But the sign is different. Instead of McBanbacks, as it's always been, it's now called Zachey's. Hmmm.

As you enter the restaurant, you are welcomed by the inviting aroma of hamburgers, potato nuggets, and desserts. You look around. "Something's different around here," you think. You can't put your finger on it. The orange plastic booths are still the same, and so are the cardboard signs that hang down from the ceiling.

But then you notice the salad bar. Last week there were three kinds of lettuce, 27 kinds of vegetables and fruit options, and lots of bread, soup, and croutons. Today you see only four pieces of lettuce, a carrot, and a paper cup with peas in it. That's all. And instead of soup, there's a bowl of water and a bottle of ketchup with these instructions: "Add ketchup to water. Stir. Enjoy tasty, homemade tomato soup."

When you approach the counter, the first thing you notice is that nobody's there. You look around...the deep fat fryer is bubbling. You look back at the door. The neon Open sign is blinking. You go back to the counter and call toward the kitchen, "Hello? Hello?"

"I'm right here—you don't have to yell," says a gruff voice from just beneath you.

"Oh, hi. Sorry, I didn't see you." You look down and down even further. Then you see the wee little man. Actually, all you can see is the top of his head.

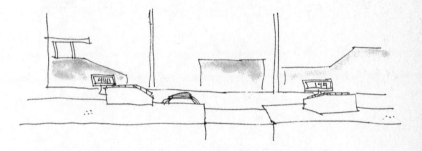

"Yeah, like I haven't heard *that* one before," he says.

This man is barely three feet tall. He's bearded and wearing an expensive-looking robe, but he can't even see over the counter. When he turns his face up to talk, you notice the deep worry line between his eyebrows and the snarl on his lips.

"So are you Zach?" you ask, wishing you had decided to have fish sticks at home.

"Yeah, short for Zacchaeus. Like I never got picked on for *that* name. And if you make any jokes about me being a short-order cook, I'll stick your hand in the fryer. Got it? Now, what can I get for you?" he asks.

"I...I guess I'll have the number three," you say, partly out of habit and partly out of fear.

"We don't serve a number three." Zach is clearly getting impatient.

"Okay...I'll have number five—a double burger, a drink, and a box of potato nuggets."

"We don't have any numbers," he says. "Or discounts. Got it?"

You silently nod because you're afraid to say anything now. This is also when you notice a small handwritten sign in the corner: Under New Management. Things are beginning to make sense. "So how long you been in business?" you ask.

"Since Wednesday. You gonna order or not?" he says, reaching up and drumming his stubby fingers on the counter.

You look up at the big menu board. There are only three choices. "Sure. Gimme one of those Tree House Burgers, tots, and a large soft drink." You glance over to where the pop machine stood on Tuesday. It's been replaced by a pitcher with a strange green liquid inside. A sign says, All you can drink—if you pay each time.

"Uh, cancel the drink," you quickly say.

"Anything else?" he asks.

"Sure, how are the cookies today?"

"Same as every day."

"Great. I'll have a cookie too." You watch his fast little fingers sail across the register.

"That'll be forty-six dollars and eighty-seven cents."

"Are you kidding? That can't be right!"

"You're right. I forgot to add the cookie. Sixty-one seventy."

You pull out your wallet. "Can I put this on my credit card?"

He points to a sign that wasn't there last week: No Checks, No Credit. Cash Only—With ID.

"Skip the cookie," you say as you lay fifty dollars in cash on the counter with your ID. You decide to find out more about this strange man. "So what did you do before you took over this place?" You say this as casually as you can.

"I worked for the government," came the short reply.

"Probably a tax collector," you guess.

"That's right, twenty-seven years with the RRS."

"The RRS?"

"The Roman Revenue Service."

You hate to ask, but the words come out anyway. "Why are your prices so high?"

"I learned that in the tax racket. Let's say at tax time you owe Rome thirty dollars."

"Yeah..."

"So I charge you sixty-five dollars. I give Rome their thirty..."

"...and keep thirty-five for yourself," you finish.

"Yep. So I do the same here. I pay the suppliers and my employee about two dollars a meal. So then I charge the customer forty-six eighty-seven."

"That's quite the markup."

"I suppose. Listen, I don't have all day," Zacchaeus said. "In fact..." He looks at the clock. "You're going to need to take your order to go." He shoos everyone out.

132

"I'm *so* not coming back here again," you say quietly as you watch him put on his coat and sneak out the kitchen back door. You're extremely curious by now, so you decide to follow the tiny restaurateur. You track him as he hobbles down a back alley.

Suddenly you hear a sound growing louder by the second. You stop and listen. What? It sounds like a crowd at a football game or a movie premiere or...or...a parade! You walk a little bit farther and see an archway that leads back to the street. Sure enough, people are lined up on both sides of the street. But instead of a parade with animals, jugglers, and fire-eating men on stilts, this event is just one guy walking down the street with a few people around him. You look more closely because now you're even more curious!

It's Jesus! No wonder everyone is trying to get a look. Even Zach is hopping up and down, leaning this way and that, trying to see Jesus. The image of him jumping makes you laugh. He's just too short. You're actually a bit surprised that your mean restaurant owner is even interested in Jesus. "The crowd is probably full of the people he ripped off," you think to yourself. But when you look back over to ask him—he's gone.

"Where did he..." Wait a second! You look up the street, and there's Zach, standing in front of a tree. "No, he's not..." but before you can finish the thought, he's climbing the tree! And for a middle-aged tax collector, the little guy is quick. You squint to see him in the tree. Zach has actually found himself a pretty good spot from which to watch Jesus and the crowd.

Zach can see the whole procession. As Jesus nears the tree, something really weird happens. Jesus and His companions stop in the middle of the street. Then Jesus looks up in the tree and says, "Hey Zacchaeus! I want to come over to your place for lunch. What's on the menu?" Zacchaeus is so surprised, he almost falls out of the tree!

You hear him call down, "Give me five minutes!" His little figure slides down the trunk and takes off running. You decide to follow. It takes you a while to work your way back to Zachey's, but you just *have* to see this!

By the time you get there, Zacchaeus is mopping the floor. "What are you doing?" you ask.

"Are you kidding? Jesus is coming to my place for lunch! I gotta get it ready!" You notice that a lot of the signs have been taken down, and the ketchup and soup stations have been removed.

Soon, Jesus arrives with His disciples. And right behind them are a whole bunch of Zach's tax collector friends as well as some pretty rough characters. Jesus invites each one to come in and sit, smiling and chatting if they had been friends for a long time. And as if that weren't amazing enough, you're even more surprised to see price-raising, profit-taking, stingy Zacchaeus paying for everyone's lunch!

Zach stands up, clinks his spoon on a water glass, and says, "Lord, I'm giving half my money to the poor. And if I've cheated anyone..."

"*If?*" the whole crowd shouts.

"Okay, okay," he corrected, "*because* I've cheated people, I'll pay them back four times as much!" Whoa, this is quite a day! Just one minute of feeling loved and accepted by Jesus, and Zacchaeus is a new man! Jesus must have really changed this guy's heart!

From that point on you decided to make Zach's Snack Shack your favorite lunch hangout.

Get Real!

Read the captivating account of Zacchaeus in Luke 19 and decide what you would have been willing to do to see Jesus back then. What do you do now to spend time with Jesus? And how does that time with Him change you in big and small ways?

What if God had a problem?

What?" you might ask. "God doesn't have problems! He's...well, He's God!"

You're absolutely right. God is perfect. He's everywhere, and He knows everything, so He could never have a problem, and nothing ever surprises Him. But God did have a couple of challenges after He created the world and people.

His first challenge was to let people know what He was like.

From the time Adam and Eve disobeyed God in the garden, people didn't walk closely with God the way Adam and Eve did in the beginning. In fact, the distance was so great, people forgot how loving and merciful God is. God wanted to remind us of what He was like...but how? Make a huge sign that stretched across the sky?

Run a commercial on all the networks at the same time?

No, God had a better idea. He realized the only way He could let people understand what He was like was to become a man and live with us on the earth for a while. So that's what He did. When Jesus was born in a stable about 2000 years ago, it was actually God Himself wrapped in those swaddling clothes and lying in the feed trough. As Jesus grew and people started to see what He was like, they started to understand what God was like. They also understood how He felt about them.

Jesus was God Himself, walking around with the rest of us. So if we want to know what God is like, we just have to look at Jesus. For example, how does God feel about kids? He loves them! Check out Luke 18:15-17. Does God want to heal our sickness and stuff? Yes! Look at Matthew 8:1-3. Will God take care for us? You bet—look up Luke 12:22-31. When you look at Jesus, you're looking at God. He even said so in John 14:8-10. What a concept!

So what was God's other challenge?

His second challenge was to draw us back to Him.

Because we do bad stuff, we can still become separated from God and His perfection. Sorry, but that's the way it is. A perfect God and imperfect people just don't mix. Even if you're a pretty good person, think back over your life. Have you ever, even for two minutes since you were born, done something bad? Selfish? Mean?

Okay, you get the picture. So our bad stuff separates us from God. It's like we're on one side of a canyon, and God's waayyyy over on the other side.

Argh! So now what do we do? Well, that was the second reason God sent His Son, Jesus, to earth—to take our place and die for us and take the punishment we deserve for all the bad stuff we've ever done. It is sort of like when Jesus died, He became a bridge for us back to the Father.

The choice is up to you—will you take the bridge back to God? Maybe you'd like to but aren't sure how. Well, you can start by saying thank You to Jesus for taking your place. Then tell God that you're sorry for the bad stuff you've done and that you'd like a new start. Ask Jesus to come into your life and start being the boss. This is what the Bible calls being "born again." You get to start over.

If you've done this, please let some people know—your parents, your pastor, or maybe your youth leader. They'll be as excited as you are!

More Great Harvest House
Books by Sandy Silverthorne

You Can Draw Bible Stories for Kids

In these short and often humorous accounts of some of the greatest Bible stories, Sandy provides simple, step-by-step instructions that show you how to create your own illustrations of various Bible characters, animals, and other objects, making each story personal and memorable. If you're between the ages of 7 and 11, this is for you!

The Awesome Book of Bible Facts

This is a storybook, first Bible dictionary, and gold mine of fascinating facts all in one. It's packed with amazing information, incredible cut-away diagrams, hundreds of illustrations, and short, easy explanations for kids like you.

101 Awesome Bible Facts for Kids

Each entry in this 144-page pocket-size fact book includes an interesting statistic, a helpful definition, or some other noteworthy morsel of data from the Old or New Testament as well as a playful cartoon illustration. These interesting facts will help you become a Bible expert in no time!

The Awesome Book About God for Kids

You'll love Alisha Braatz's thoroughly up-to-date retellings of stories from the Bible. Each one highlights an important aspect of God's nature. With brief applications and Sandy Silverthorne's delightful cartoon drawings, this collection is perfect for you to enjoy on your own or with adults by your side.

One-Minute Mysteries and Brain Teasers

Return of the One-Minute Mysteries and Brain Teasers

Mind-Boggling One-Minute Mysteries and Brain Teasers

Your entire family will be astonished and stumped by these interactive mysteries. In brief paragraphs and black-and-white illustrations, Sandy joins John Warner in presenting puzzles with logical, "aha" answers that require thinking outside the box. Clues and answers are included in separate sections. Hours of wholesome entertainment is practically guaranteed!